It's fun to draw

Sea Creatures

Mark Bergin

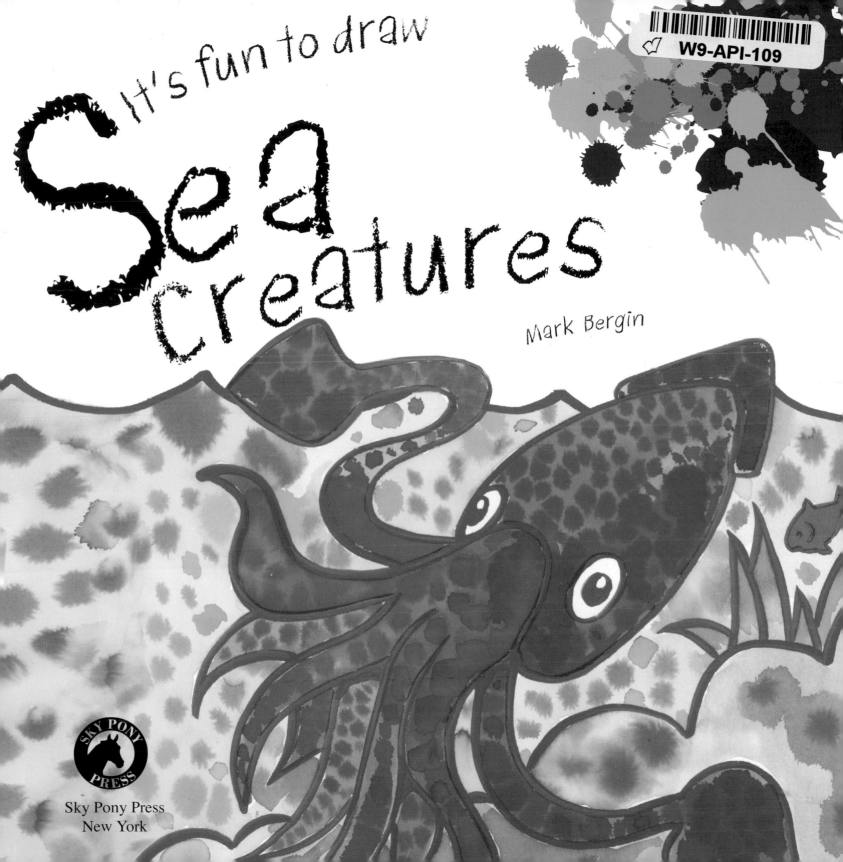

Sky Pony Press
New York

Author:
Mark Bergin was born in Hastings, England. He
has illustrated an award-winning series and written
over twenty books. He has done many book
designs, layouts, and storyboards in many styles
including cartoon for numerous books, posters, and
advertisements. He lives in Bexhill-on-sea with his
wife and three children.

HOW TO USE THIS BOOK:
Start by following the numbered splats on the left-
hand page. These steps will ask you to add some
lines to your drawing. The new lines are always
drawn in red so you can see how the drawing
builds from step to step. Read the "You can do it!"
splats to learn about drawing and shading
techniques you can use.

First published in the UK by The Salaryia Book Company ©
The Salaryia Book Company Limited 2012.

Sky Pony Press books may be purchased in bulk at special
discounts for sales promotion, corporate gifts, fund-raising, or
educational purposes. Special editions can also be created to
specifications. For details, contact the Special Sales Department,
Sky Pony Press, 307 West 36th Street, 11th Floor, New York,
NY 10018 or info@skyhorsepublishing.com.

Sky Pony® is a registered trademark of Skyhorse Publishing,
Inc.®, a Delaware corporation.

Visit our website at www.skyponypress.com.

10 9 8 7 6 5 4 3 2 1

Manufactured in China, March 2013
This product conforms to CPSIA 2008

Library of Congress Cataloging-in-Publication Data
Bergin, Mark, 1961-
[Sea creatures]
It's fun to draw sea creatures / Mark Bergin.
pages cm
Includes index.
ISBN 978-1-62087-535-3 (pbk. : alk. paper)
1. Marine animals in art--Juvenile literature. 2. Drawing--
Technique--Juvenile literature. I. Title.
NC781.B47 2013
743.6--dc23
2013010379

ISBN: 978-1-62087-535-3

Contents

Coral reef fish

1 Start with a circle for the body.

2 Add two large fin shapes and a tail.

3 Draw in the head and mouth. Add a small fin.

4 Draw in the eye and add a stripy pattern.

splat-a-fact

These fish are colorful and live near coral reefs.

5

Crab

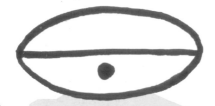

1 Start with an oval for the body. Add a line and a dot for the mouth.

2 Add two eyes on stalks.

splat-a-fact

Crabs walk sideways.

you can do it!

Draw the lines with a blue felt-tip marker. Use colored felt-tip markers to add color.

3 Draw in the claws; one is much larger than the other.

4 Add eight legs.

Dolphin

1 Start with a banana-shaped body.

 2 Draw in the tail, and add a fin.

3 Add two more fins and the body marking.

splat-a-fact

Dolphins are mammals and breathe air, just like you do.

you can do it!

Draw in the lines with a blue felt-tip marker. Add color using colored pencils.

4 Draw in an eye, and finish off the mouth.

Manta ray

1 Start by drawing the shape of the body.

2 Draw in two curved shapes at the front. Draw in the mouth.

3 Add lines for the gills and a pointed tail.

you can do it!

Cut up tissue paper and glue it down to make interesting textures.

4 Draw in the eyes.

10

Octopus

 1 Start by drawing a circle for the head.

 2 Draw four curly tentacles.

splat-a-fact
Octopuses have 8 tentacles and live in rocky shores and tidepools.

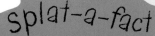 **3** Add two more tentacles.

4 Draw in two more tentacles. Add dots for eyes.

Flying fish

1 Start with a
banana-shaped body.

2 Add an eye, a line
for the gill, and
a tail fin.

splat-a-fact

Flying fish make
long, flying leaps
out of the water.

you can do it!

Use colored pencils
and smudge them with
your finger. Draw the
lines with a felt-tip
marker.

3 Draw in two large fins.

4 Add four smaller fins.

Marlin

splat-a-fact
Marlins are fish with a long body, a spear-like snout, and a long fin on their back.

2 Add a curved body and a tail fin.

1 Start with the head shape. Add a dot for the eye.

you can do it!
Use watercolor paint to color. Use a sponge to dab on more paint for added texture. Use a felt-tip marker for the lines.

4 Add smaller fins.

3 Draw in a long, curved back fin.

Puffer fish

you can do it!
Use colored pencils and a felt-tip marker for the lines. Use scribbly lines to color in.

1 Start with a spiky shape.

2 Add a mouth and two dots for eyes.

3 Draw in two striped gills.

4 Add a tail fin and spikes.

splat-a-fact

Puffer fish are the second-most poisonous vertebrate in the world.

18

Sea horse

1 Start with the head. Add a dot for the eye.

2 Draw in the curved body with a curly tail.

you can do it!

Use crayons for texture, and then paint over with watercolor paint.

3 Add a spiky fin on the back.

4 Add spikes from its head to its tail.

Splat-a-fact

There are nearly 50 species of sea horse.

Seal

you can do it!
Use colored inks and a felt-tip marker for the lines.

1 Start with a circle for the head.

2 Draw in two eyes, a nose, and a mouth.

3 Add curved lines for the body.

Splat-a-fact
Seals can hold their breath underwater for nearly two hours.

4 Draw in two spiky flippers.

5 Add two spiky fins.

Whale

1 Start by cutting out the whale shape. Add a dot for the eye.

you can do it!
Glue down candy wrappers for the sea and torn white paper for the clouds.

MAKE SURE YOU GET AN ADULT TO HELP YOU WHEN USING SCISSORS!

2 Use a felt-tip marker to draw in the mouth and a blowhole.

3 Cut out the shape of the mouth from colored paper. Glue it down.

splat-a-fact
To breathe, whales have a blowhole in the top of their heads.

shark

1 Start with the body shape.

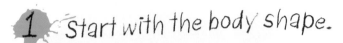

2 Add the tail fin.

3 Draw in two large fins and three smaller fins.

4 Add an angry eye, lines for the gills, and jagged teeth.

26

Squid

1 Start with an oval for the head. Add the mantle.

2 Draw in the eyes.

3 Draw in four arms using curved lines.

4 Add another four arms. Draw two long tentacles with heart shapes at the end.

you can do it!

Color with watercolor paint. Add ink to the sea and the body while the paint is still wet.

Turtle

1 Start with a round shape for the body.

2 Add the head and beak.

Splat-a-fact
Turtles lived 100 million years ago—in the age of dinosaurs.

3 Draw in the arm flippers and back legs.

4 Draw in the eyes and beak shape. Add the pattern to the shell.

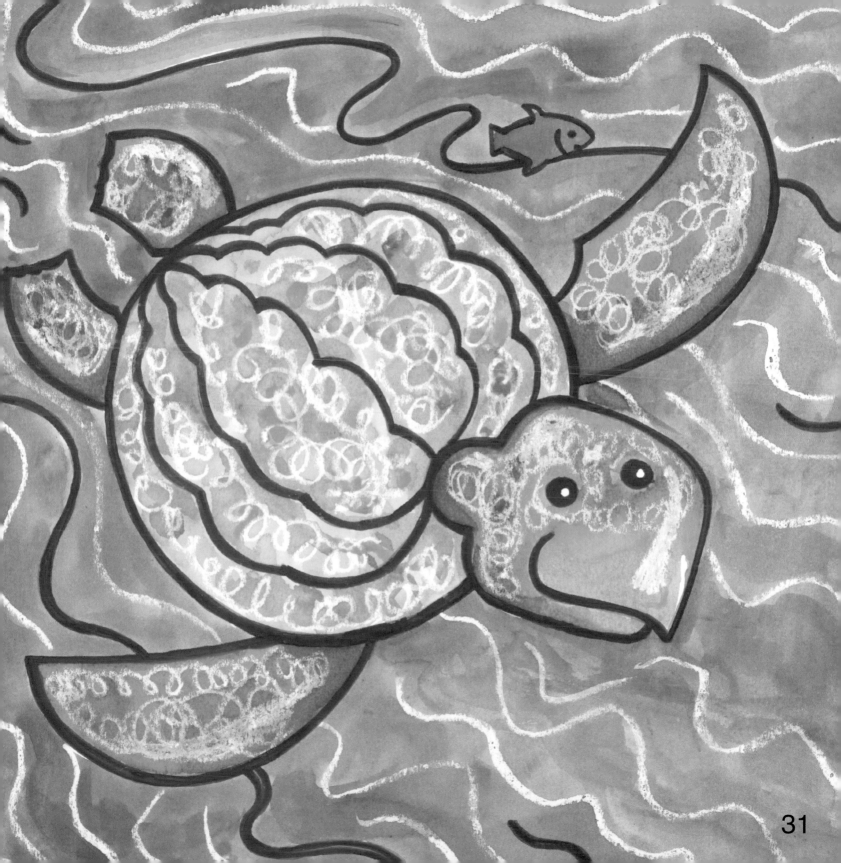

Index